Don Quixotic

BEN GREENMAN

ANTIBOOKCLUB
NEW YORK

Some of these stories have previously appeared in print, in different forms. Stories 1 and 43 appeared in *Scoundrel Time*; stories 21, 86, and 87 appeared in *Zyzzyva*.

Cover design by ANTIBOOKCLUB
Book design by Will Petty

ISBN: 978-0-9838683-4-7

Library of Congress Control Number: 2017947586

Printed in the United States of America

10 9 8 7 6 2 3 4 5

To Uncle Sam—both the symbol and the eagle.

Author's Note

I wrestled with this book. I continue to wrestle with it. These pieces were mostly written in the last months of 2016 and the first months of 2017. During that time, President Trump was clownish. He was crass. He was misogynistic and xenophobic, a bully and a boor, always narcissistic, never noble, always a salesman, never a statesman. Still, throughout his campaign and the first months of this administration, many Americans held out hope that the gravity of the office would improve him somewhat, that he would learn to represent all Americans—or at least that he would appeal to the nation's sometimes elusive better nature.

Then came August 2017, and the Unite the Right march in Charlottesville, Virginia, which brought together alt-right and white supremacist groups under the pretext of opposing the removal of a statue of Robert E. Lee. The marchers staged a Friday night event complete with torches and were out in force Saturday as well, where they were met by protestors. One of those anti-racist protestors, a thirty-two-year-old woman named Heather Heyer, was in a crowd that was struck by a car driven by a young man who had come to Charlottesville to attend the white supremacist rally. She was killed. Others were injured.

In the days that followed, Trump not only refused to clearly condemn the racist groups that had gathered in Charlottesville, but seemed to legitimize them, suggesting that they were only part of the problem. A tepid set of remarks delivered on Saturday (Trump said, and then repeated, that there was violence "on many sides") was followed by a stiffly read statement on Monday and in turn obliterated by a wild press conference on Tuesday. There, Trump again split the blame between both sides, refusing to acknowledge that only one side had instigated, that only one side had openly advocated a terrifying racism. A president who never bothered with nuance insisted that the situation was nuanced. A president who never bothered waiting for facts before reacting said that he had held back judgment because he was waiting for facts. Whatever moral authority the president might have had—whatever moral authority an uneasy nation needed him to have—was swept away in a tide of toxic wrongheadedness. Both Democrats and Republicans decried the president's Tuesday remarks as a bridge too far. Many suggested that he was winking at the white nationalists who had helped to elect him, and in fact many of the leaders of that movement agreed, taking comfort in the president's delayed and equivocal criticism.

Months from now, years from now, August may prove to be a turning point in the Trump presidency. His support may dwindle rapidly. He may retreat further inside paranoia and rage. It's hard to say. I'm trapped here in August. We don't even know how the Russia investigation is going to end. And this book, written as Trump secured the GOP nomination, as he campaigned against and then defeated Hillary Clinton in the general election, is trapped in its time, attempting to explore the unprecedented phenomenon of this strange, maladjusted, bull-in-china-shop, legend-in-his-own-mind president, this disproportionately rewarded fool. It uses comedy and fantasy, philosophical speculation and psychological ventriloquism. But is the offensive, bungling, worrisome, faintly laughable Donald Trump of the fall of 2016 still with us, or has he metastasized into something even darker and uglier? And what will happen now?

Again, this book does not know. It cannot know. Books are never finished. They are only abandoned. I now abandon this one to publication. Outside of these pages, life will go on, and for a while at least it will go on with this erratic demagogue occupying the nation's highest office. Like everyone else, I will wait and I will watch, but I will not allow myself to worry. As Corrie ten Boom wrote, "Worry does not empty tomorrow of its sorrow. It empties today of its strength."

Ben Greenman
August 2017

1

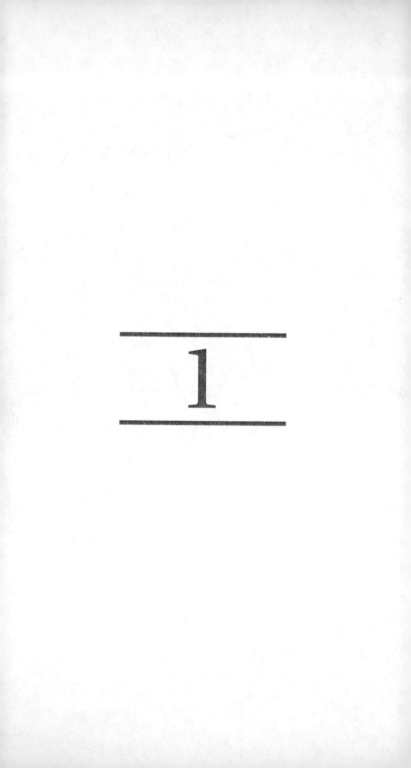

The man, newly chosen, newly elected, walked down the street. It was not a street. It was a hallway in a building he owned. He owned many other buildings, though many of them he did not own. Those other buildings were owned by other men. Those other men knew it was to their advantage to put the man's name on those other buildings, so that other people would notice them. The man would go to any length to ensure that things with his name on them were noticed, no matter the cost. Thus the placing of his name on things initiated a cycle. The man believed the cycle was virtuous. It was a cycle but not virtuous. It was a hallway but not a street. The buildings were owned but not owned. The man walked down the street of the building, acknowledging these contradictions not at all.

2

The mystery of birth did not interest him. He got born. That was all he needed to know. "I'll take it from here," he said, though he said it much later, as the punch line to a joke, though his birth was not a joke but rather a serious matter that changed the course of the world, though he said the thing about taking it from here long before he changed the course of the world, though he always knew he would.

3

Voodoo wasn't real. It was a superstition, even less real than his own religion, which wasn't real either. You couldn't put a pin in a doll and break a faraway foot or neck. But he did believe a version of it, which is that if he had angry thoughts about someone and focused those thoughts into a laser-like beam, harm would come to that person, even if that harm was only his own anger. And he did think of other people as small dolls to be stuck with pins.

4

He understood many phrases. He understood them all. Of course he did. Any extremely smart person would. The only one he didn't understand was "born with a silver spoon in his mouth." Why was that so great? Silver spoons were all over the place: in drawers, in soup bowls, in desserts. Gold spoons were another matter. He hoped one day to see a baby born with a gold spoon in its mouth. He hoped one day to hold that baby and see his own features in its face.

5

A boy who sat near him in school started saying that money didn't matter, that it wasn't everything, and another boy said that it was a resource that could be used to power anything, even emotions, and a third boy said that there was a difference between money and value, and a fourth boy said that currency was a metaphor. He checked his watch. While they were blathering, his father had made eighty thousand dollars, and at least some of that would be coming his way.

6

Sundays were perfectly suited for meditation and contemplation, for a measured consideration of the events of the week that had just passed, for a private reckoning where a man could admit error and pledge to be better in the days to come. Sundays were a haven of silence and succor, a place of honesty and humility. Sundays were days where men came to terms with their own insignificance, and the ways in which that conferred a broader significance upon them. He hated Sundays.

7

He won. He won so much. And though his brother liked to joke that he won so much because he only played alone, that was a lie. He won so much because he was better. He won at football. He won at baseball. He won at golf. Anything that involved moving a body through space, he was a prohibitive favorite. A soccer coach pulled him aside one afternoon. He had just scored a goal. “You’re good at this,” coach said. “But this won’t translate into anything unless you see it a certain way.” It was like a door had opened in the air before his eyes. He thanked the man. He had thanked many adults, but this time he meant it.

8

As a child, he was capable of love and rage in equal measure. As he grew older, one of those things receded from him and he grew expert at falsifying it, though he did not make a practice of acknowledging which one of the two it was, even to himself, and one day, beginning to raise his voice to a girlfriend who had not called him back promptly, he realized that he had forgotten.

9

He worked at his father's feet while his father was on the phone. He had wooden blocks he made into buildings. "Look," he said to his father. His father did not. His father stayed on the phone. He stayed at his father's feet. He made higher and higher towers with the blocks. His father never looked.

10

“Each of you should write down the thing that interests you the most,” the teacher said. She was a young brunette who wore her hair in a bun. One of the things that interested him the most was imagining how she looked with her hair down. A girl behind him shifted in her seat and he could hear the swish of skirt on leg. That interested him, too. Outside the window, cars drove by, cars driven by powerful men who had bid goodbye to wives and were on their way to see girlfriends. The cars gleamed. He was only in ninth grade but he understood the entire world. The teacher coughed to remind the class of the assignment. “Undiscovered planets,” he wrote down, telling the truth.

11

The first woman he ever saw undressing was a tall blonde who braided her hair once she was naked. She was the older sister of a friend from school. He was visiting the family, and she invited him upstairs after dinner and before dessert, and they kissed a little, and she asked him if he minded if she changed. “No,” he said. She shook her head. “You should have said something funny, like ‘Don’t ever change,’” she said. He didn’t think it was a good time for a joke. He was dead serious. He tapped his watch to show her that they were short on time.

12

He loved watching football. His smart son-in-law said it was because there were winners and losers, and he agreed and said that was the reason, but it wasn't. He was happy for the winners, but they weren't what attracted him to the games. What attracted him were the losers: quarterbacks who threw the ball away at the wrong moment, running backs who got stopped at the line, coaches with looks of stupid frustration on their face. He loved watching all of that because he liked to imagine that he was the one causing the errors and the frustrated faces. For every loser, there was a winner standing over that loser gloating, and he imagined he was every winner. He also had a soft spot for injuries.

13

The end of a year was the beginning of a year. People were okay with that. Time passed. And yet, when he said things that sounded like contradictions, people got mad. It didn't seem right. What did time have that he didn't have?

14

People were the same wherever you went, in that they were different wherever you went but shared certain key traits, one being that many of them could easily be fooled with loud noises and shiny things put forward by manipulators, and that if you got to those people, the few remaining people who couldn't be fooled no matter how loud the noises and how shiny the things didn't matter very much for very long, because the same temperament that kept those few remaining people from being fooled by loud noises and shiny things kept them from making loud noises and flashing shiny things, and as a result they couldn't wrest the many from your grasp, to the point where it didn't even matter if you accidentally got lost in the thicket of your thought and admitted you were in fact the manipulator in question, wherever you went.

15

“Don’t do anything the old way. Don’t do anything the way other people want you to. Don’t do anything that requires you to think too hard about the needs of people you weren’t thinking about a moment before, or people you haven’t met yet. Whatever’s left over, well, you can do that.” Most people couldn’t have fit that on a bumper sticker, but his car was huge.

16

On the nights when the late-night shows weren't funny (which was every night, if you asked him), he would send Mike out to scavenge a refrigerator box from the sidewalk, and then he would have Chris paint it to look like a television set, one of the old console models, with a square cutout for the screen, and then he would walk around behind it and do his own comedy show. Most of his jokes and skits were about how great he was and how all his decisions were perfect. They found a receptive audience in Mike and Chris, who laughed at every single part and sat as long as the show ran, never even getting up to go to the bathroom.

17

When he was very young, a friend of his father's he didn't much care for tried to get into his good graces by telling him a bedtime story. "Once there was a frog who wanted to be bigger than every other frog," the man said. "He was also afraid of every other frog, so the only frog he would look at was the frog in his mirror. But he wasn't bigger than that frog. He was the same size. He puffed himself up and puffed himself up. Still, he was only the same size as the frog in the mirror, so he puffed himself up some more. He felt his skin straining. He felt pressure at his eyes. Nothing seemed to work. The frog in the mirror was still his size. He took one more deep breath, and that was his last breath. People outside the house heard the popping noise." It wasn't until years later that it occurred to him that the man had been making a point. He knew he had been right to dislike the guy in the first place.

18

He was with Steve in the pet store, standing near a cage with three cats in it, not saying anything about the cats, but just standing there near the cage, staring. Two of the cats were black and one was white. One of the two black cats had been injured in some way and couldn't open one of its eyes. That half-blind cat was the oldest of the three. The other two were young, not quite kittens anymore but not yet battle-scarred. He noticed the one white cat kept its distance from the two black cats, and he wondered if Steve noticed the same thing. He almost said something about it, but what would he say? A joke? Would he make a wise noise? He never had cats when he was a kid. Didn't like them very much. Wasn't a huge fan of pets at any rate. All they did was eat up space and money. They made messes. And though they pretended they loved you, they couldn't say so, and it was the saying so that mattered. He watched the cats in the cage. The old black one got up and walked over to the white one. They stood nose to nose, nuzzling. He wondered if Steve noticed. Now he really didn't know what to say. He turned with force so Steve would turn, too. They bought a chew toy for Steve's dog and hit the road. There was a meeting on strategic partnerships coming up at noon. It was nearly noon.

19

He had a special way he watched awards shows. When they announced nominees, he silently added in his own name, and then when they announced a winner, he spoke his own name aloud. The name they said out loud was usually a different name, which was what led to his theory that the awards were rigged. He went into the election with the same philosophy, but that time the name they said was the same as the name he was saying. He stood and walked forward to accept the award, not realizing he was at home until his head bumped the TV screen.

20

There were many moments in the middle of it all when he wished that time would stop—or, if not stop, move only slightly ahead, and then slightly back, and then slightly ahead, and then slightly back, going over the same small patch of triumph, wearing it thin perhaps, but never surrendering to the actual future, which was filled with the unknown, with challenge, with change, with peril.

21

He made mazes for others because he feared them himself. He suffered from a terror of the labyrinth. When there were things that he couldn't understand, he felt his heart begin to race away from him. That was why he expressed one thing and then its opposite. That was why he did not express one thing and then its opposite. That was why he clouded the air and vowed never to cloud it. He wanted others to be in the same spot, in the same fix, unable to decide which way to turn, dead-ended, drowning in their own dread.

22

During dessert—a ring of dark chocolate around a small orange ball, and then around that a larger disk of white chocolate, the whole thing too complicated to look at, let alone eat—his eye kept drifting to the back of the restaurant, where there was a brick fireplace, and a fire, and next to the fire a beautiful brunette who kept checking her watch. She is waiting for me, he thought. When I walk up to her table, she will smile at me, he thought. He could barely pay attention to what his father and mother were saying. He kicked himself for not noticing her earlier in the meal. And so, when dessert was cleared, when coffee was on the way, he walked to the back of the restaurant and stood next to the young woman's table. "Are you waiting for me?" he said. She shook her head. She had been striking from far away and was even more so up close. Her hair was like a vinyl record. "No," she said. She smiled at him but not the way he wanted her to. "I'm waiting for the most powerful man in the world." Fifty years later, when he became that man, he thought of that woman. She was probably old now and hard to look at.

23

Concert pianists impressed him. Their hands flew across their instrument, leaving behind both structure and beauty, but only for a moment, and then that, too, flew away. They impressed him partly because he couldn't do what they did. He thought about learning how to do it. He knew he would have a flair for the dramatic, at least. Over time, it became clear that learning how to do it was too difficult, so instead he learned not to be impressed by them.

24

Yes, yes, people said that all people were equal, that women could be as smart and talented as men, that everyone, regardless of race or ethnicity or the wealth of their parents, possessed a capacity for brilliance and sensitivity, as well as the potential to succeed in nearly any field. That's what people said, but what did they really believe? That was the question that truly interested him, not because the answer hurt others—he wasn't a monster—but because it helped him.

25

There was one doorman he liked tussling with, a little guy, Puerto Rican, had seemed ancient for twenty years, didn't do the normal routine, yes sir, of course sir, let me get that for you sir, instead told him how he was feeling that day, maybe one day his back was killing him, another day he couldn't shake a cold, that honesty was rare in a doorman, rare and valuable, an unexpected moment of human connection, a shot back into the days when he was working for his father on those first buildings in Queens, and Ramon was that way to him now, and so he was that way to Ramon, a little jab here and there to keep the old guy sharp, and every holiday season they had a joke between them that when he tipped Ramon he was paying back a loan, and so the hundred came out of the money clip with an apology, "Sorry I'm late, I fell a little behind," and Ramon played the whole thing straight, never even cracking a smile, and he was left to get the door himself, because on tip days Ramon wouldn't open it for him, and when the cold November air hit his face he had a surge of freedom he rarely felt anymore, and he thought mainly what a bargain that was, just a hundred lousy bucks for freedom. There was one doorman he liked tussling with, a little guy, Puerto Rican.

26

When he was young, he saw *Dog Day Afternoon* on a second date. Afterwards, at a bar, the woman kept talking about how Sonny was a hero because he was trying to help his boyfriend, and how the cops were a mess, all disorganized and violent and quick to make mistakes. He didn't say anything. The woman leaned back in her chair. She looked a little like Jacqueline Bisset: same perfect mouth. "You probably identify with the cops," she said, taking a long drag on her cigarette. She didn't know what she was talking about. He identified with the bank.

27

As a little boy, he was visiting one of his father's buildings when an old man appeared as if by magic in the hallway and gave him some advice he would keep close to his heart for the rest of his life. "When you fail," the old man said, "say you succeeded. When you succeed, say you succeeded even more. When you don't know something, say that you do. When you have doubts, hide them." There was no old man. He had just pulled back his lips over his teeth to make his mouth seem like a gummy old man's mouth, pulled back his hair on his forehead to make his head look like a bald old man's head, looked at his reflection in a window, and given himself the advice. By the time his father had returned, the old man had vanished.

28

He did not take orders from anyone except the universe itself, and even then it was only one order: Proceed, proceed.

29

He revered ancient military leaders like Alacandro the Visigoth, Barnaby the Great, Scipio of Antioch, Klobus, Probus, Myron of Athens, Ozilius Philippius Sicilius, Heptimus Haroldus, and Prince Tanaranana, and it didn't bother him one bit that he had made them all up.

30

When the auction for coffee with his daughter first went up, he considered bidding on it himself. He would love to have coffee with her. He didn't get to see her enough. He mentioned it to her during their daily lunch and she laughed and told him that he didn't even drink coffee. That evening, during their daily phone call, he told her that he would have settled for tea or even Postum. "What the hell is Postum?" she said. "Tell you at breakfast," he said.

31

There was something he was forgetting. "If you can't remember something," his father used to say, "it's not worth remembering." His father called him a prince, which meant that his father was the king. That went without saying. "Never forget," his father said. "You come first and others come last." He spat the word "others." The king gave fatherly advice every day, right up until the point when he sent the prince away. "It's a good school," his father said. "We'll talk." But when he would call home, his father was too busy to get on the phone. "Work first," the king would say. He not only said it, but he lived it. It was inspiring to see a man live the things he said. The king was gone now. The prince remembers how he had loved him, and how he had mostly only wanted to hear his voice a little longer. He had forgotten that there were other things he was forgetting.

32

It could not be his room. Someone was playing a trick on him. It had to be his sister's room or his brother's room or his other brother's room or his other sister's room. It didn't suit him. It was too small. The light was bad. The wall had peeling paper. There was a window that looked directly into the window of a hospital, where he could see sick people moving slowly through space. He sat on the bed all afternoon, on into the evening, fuming, silently cursing his parents, silently hoping someone would come in and tell him a mistake had been made. When it was dark outside, he turned on all the lights in the room and looked at his reflection on the inside of the window. He made different expressions, all of which had the same meaning, which was that he refused to imagine either the peeling wall behind him or the sick people in front of him.

33

Early to bed and early to rise makes a man healthy, wealthy, and wise. But also: securing the services of an eccentric doctor who allowed you to furnish a description of your own mental and physical condition, after which he simply signed the letter; parlaying your father's business successes into your own, taking advantage of various loopholes along the way, not infrequently stiffing contractors; and letting thoughts fly from mind to mouth like agitated canaries looking for the opening of a cage—those things, as it turned out, could just as easily make a man healthy, wealthy, and wise.

34

In his mid-forties, he became obsessed with a TV program that showed ordinary people humiliated via slapstick. They slipped and fell down stairs. They rolled off beds. They stepped on rakes, which came rapidly to attention, striking them in the face. Rakes! The world was so full of peril, and that peril was so full of entertainment value. Ordinarily, he never laughed—not at comedians that everyone insisted were hilarious, not at jokes when jokes were told, not even at the funny papers, which were papers, certainly, but not funny—but when he sat down in front of that show and a little boy came dashing around a corner in the dead of winter and went ass over teakettle on a patch of ice, he let loose with such a great torrent of laughter that his wife, a proper Southern belle, ran into the room to see what was wrong. He imagined ice in the doorway and that only made him laugh louder.

35

"Such horrible things were said about him so consistently that a lesser man might have begun to believe that some of them were true." He had either read that somewhere or he had imagined that he had. "Such wonderful things were said about him so consistently that a greater man would have begun to believe that some of them were false." That he had never read anywhere. It didn't make any sense at all. A greater man? What could that even mean?

36

Whenever he attended a party, he made a bet with himself that he could get the most attractive person in the room to talk to him. And so, immediately after he arrived, he would check his coat, find the first person he knew, start up a conversation, excuse himself from it, hurry to the restroom, and stand in front of the mirror. "Hi there," he'd say, winning the bet.

37

Wasn't all news fake, when it came down to it? Many events that people believed had happened had not really happened. There were entire books, holy books, that served as perfect examples. And so many events that people didn't believe had in fact happened. Spies had stolen lightly along wires, collecting information that did not belong to them, trading it for money or power or more information. You told people that and they scoffed. The more serious your expression, the more they thought they were being had. Perhaps they were comforting themselves. Maybe they couldn't imagine such a thing. At any rate, there were enough of those cases, both cases where things that were not true were believed and cases where things that were true were not believed, that it was all fake. News, like anything fragile, was bound to shatter when it encountered human minds.

38

Corporate logos obsessed him. Why did NBC get the peacock? Why didn't he get it? Shouldn't there be some commission that determined who best represented the qualities of a particular animal or shape? It was big government, but it would have been worth it, because it would have returned the brilliant fan of feathers to its rightful home, spreading out majestically over the U in his name.

39

Every parody of him missed his essential characteristics, which were that he was good at everything, great at some things, bad at nothing, could learn anything. He could write a much better parody. He could write a fantastic one. He wouldn't get tripped up once. He had never written a parody but he knew he could do it. He was golfing when he had this realization, using a four iron at the par-three eleventh, and he hit his drive a perfect one hundred and eighty-eight yards right into the cup, hole in one. That should go in the parody, he thought.

40

Gradually he got used to living in the sky, high above the rest of the city, and he came to terms with the fact that he did not mind if it struck other people as a metaphor for status, or power, or merit, or anything else for that matter.

41

Taxes made him think of tariffs, and tariffs made him think of Tenerife, and Tenerife made him think of canaries, and canaries made him think of eagles, and eagles made him think of America, and America made him think of "No Taxation Without Representation," and "No Taxation Without Representation" made him think of taxes, and that's how he spent the morning, his mind a snow globe of phrases, until eventually most of them settled and a joke surfaced. "The difference is that I had a canary once and I released that," he said. Chris, sitting at his elbow, laughed like a hyena, even though he had no context for the remark. You could always count on Chris.

42

He closed his eyes and tried to guess what time it was. It had been four fifteen a few minutes before, when he was tweeting about how newspapers were failures. Four fifteen in the morning? He opened his eyes and looked at the clock. Wrong answer! It was four twenty-six. He closed his eyes and tried to guess again. Four twenty-six? He opened his eyes. So true!

43

Long before he was in politics, there was another guy who was in politics who said that there are known knowns, which are things that we know we know; known unknowns, which are things that we know we do not know; and unknown unknowns, which are things that we don't even know that we do not know. Everyone made such a big deal when the guy said it. They thought it made a ton of sense but also made no sense. His smart son-in-law said it was "quote considered either a masterpiece of post-modern epistemology or a master class in political evasion unquote." His smart son-in-law actually said the quote and unquote out loud, which probably meant that it was something that someone else had said or written and that he was repeating. Personally, he didn't see what was so master anything about the quote. He didn't agree with it. For him, there were only known knowns, and then a whole bunch of garbage piled outside the door. He snapped off two squares of the chocolate bar he was holding and ate them, not one square after the other but both at once.

44

The main talent he had wasn't business or building. It was charm. He could get anyone to like him at least a little, especially as they learned that they disliked him because of statements he had made but not meant. Do you hate the fish for being slippery, or admire its scales? He thought that might come in handy after he was elected. He could charm the leader of a foreign power whose friendship had long eluded America. He could smooth over wrinkles. And if he determined that the other leader was in fact an enemy, he could bring the man closer and closer—and then grab the man by the neck and, muscles bulging, personally dismiss him from his earthly existence. In the movie that ran continuously in his head, this was one of the most exciting parts.

45

He would never tell anyone why he wore his tie long, which was that he had been on the toilet, bored, when he spotted his son's mythology textbook on the gold shelf next to the throne. He picked the book up and flipped through it, grumbling about how much money he was wasting on this so-called education when he could just bring his kids to his office and teach them everything. Then he came to the part about the Fates, and Atropos snipping the thread of life. He gasped. From that day on, he wore his ties long. But he would never tell anyone the reason. Let them think it was a phallic thing, overcompensation, bad fashion, whatever. Let them think anything but what it was.

46

He tried to stay calm. He tried to stay calm and still somehow feel drama all around him. He tried to feel drama all around him as a way of keeping energy levels elevated. He tried to keep energy levels elevated because if they fell below a certain point it seemed like a form of death. He tried to hold death at bay variously, by traveling, by speaking, by building. He made money and stacked it between himself and death. All this was written on a list he kept in a blue leather book in the top drawer of his bedside table. It was mahogany, the table. When he was adding to the list in the blue leather book, his wife came up to him and started talking about a trip they were taking to Florida. She went on for a while about the trip and what she planned to do on it. He tried to stay calm. "You come right up to me," he said, "and start right in, but I am thinking. I have thoughts." He put that on the list, too: He had thoughts.

47

Once, after eating dinner at one of the world's most expensive restaurants and sleeping in one of the world's most expensive hotels, he was leaving town on a jet he owned, nibbling on the corner of a pastry, when he looked down at his shirtfront and saw a spatter of crumbs. He laughed. "Ha," he said out loud. It amused him a man of his wealth and stature could, like any other man, like a far poorer man, look down at his shirtfront and see a spatter of crumbs. Maybe there was no difference. He started to brush the crumbs away but stopped. That was the difference. A poorer man had to brush them away to feel better about his life. He looked up, away from the crumbs, into the cabin of the jet he owned. A stewardess, for the moment clothed, was coming up the aisle, smiling almost as if she was paid to do it.

48

If you said one thing, people were likely to believe it. If you said two things that were in direct conflict with one another, people wouldn't know what to believe. They would try to believe both but would end up believing neither, which would create for you a sort of vacuum that served as an opportunity. People would not know the proper manner in which to disbelieve you, and you would no longer be held in place by the irritating question of whether or not you were believed. This was a surefire strategy. It never worked. See?

49

One day he indexed his mind. The longest continuous stretch of time was devoted to thinking of his eldest daughter: seventy-two minutes of solid thought, plus eleven other fleeting moments where she skated across his mind but did not stop to be fully seen. His wife got forty-two minutes, plus seven surfacings in stories primarily about others; his eldest son, twenty-six; his middle son, twenty; his youngest son, fourteen; his other daughter, eleven. He himself got the largest amount of thought, though it was not continuous; he returned to the subject of himself over and over again across the course of the day, more than two hundred minutes total. The strategist and the campaign manager came up in a half-dozen places each, as did his mother and father, the previous president, and his defeated opponent; the doorman in four; and the driver in two. There was no evidence of having thought of his other employees, his investors in distant lands, the press (this surprised him!), or his voting public.

50

"Hello," he said into the phone. "This is Maverick. The fox is in the henhouse." No answer. "Hello," he said. "This is Maverick. The stopper is in the tub." No answer. "Hello," he said. "The egg is in the carton. The farmer is in the dell. The mountain is in the painting. The spoon is in the borscht." Still no answer. "I read you loud and clear," he said, and hung up. His daughter was just passing by the doorway. "Who was that?" she said. He angled his head toward the phone. "That was the boss," he said. "Don't be silly, Daddy," she said, laughing. "You're the boss."

51

He had one rule: When he was on a bus, he could say whatever he wanted. He had two rules: When he was on a bus he could say whatever he wanted, and when he spoke in front of crowds he could rouse them to anger but pretend later that their anger was only innocent enthusiasm. He had three rules: When he was on a bus he could say whatever he wanted, and when he spoke in front of crowds he could rouse them to anger but pretend later that their anger was only innocent enthusiasm, and he could take people's money in exchange for services without delivering those services. He had one rule: He would never limit himself to a set number of rules.

52

The snow was coming down. “Winter,” he said, not with any particular tone. His smart son-in-law came running around the corner. “It is winter,” he said. “But you know, there are parts of the world where it’s summer.” He started laughing. What a wonderful joke, to pretend that there were places where people had different perspectives and experienced different things. He laughed so hard that Chris and Rudy started laughing, too. You could always count on them to have the exact same sense of humor. They were both great guys, except maybe Chris.

53

"And so," the article concluded, "the nation is left to wonder about his ability to make decisions about the fundamental questions that face us—and, moreover, decisions that do not change with the wind." He was hungry. Barbecue, great. Burgers, great. Squash, awful. Bananas, gross. Macaroni and cheese, a big zero. Walnuts, stupid. Beans, weak. Avocados, winner. Applesauce, winner. Artichokes, loser. Popcorn, terrific. Hot sauce, tremendous. Chocolate-covered raisins, real nice. Beef jerky, tough, smart. Balut, out of control. None of that was changing with the wind, no matter how it blew.

54

Listen: One question was what things meant, not individual things but everything, what the point was and what the purpose of locating the point might one day be. Another question was how to contend with the suffering that took the form of boredom that seemed everywhere in the modern world, technology having pretended to help humanity when in fact it had trapped and tranquilized it. A third question was whether the language itself had been pitched down a well. He sketched out these questions on a napkin and then crumpled it up and threw it away. They were questions for other people, and sensitivity to them was a liability that could not be countenanced He got into the elevator, which went up or down, no questions asked. It was an elevator for strong people.

55

Think about the grape. It could be a normal fruit on a vine or it could be changed into alcohol, which ruined men's minds, had ruined his brother's mind, was something that he avoided religiously, even though he wasn't a religious man, or rather was a religious man, loved the Bible, hung on its every word, opened himself to each verse and rhyme, let the faith course through him, but that was not the point, the point was the grape, and how innocent it could seem before it ruined men's minds, and how it was the same way with many other things, with power, with money, to the point where he had learned early on that these were things that he had to master so that they wouldn't master him. He popped a green grape into his mouth, got it before it could get him, before it could be changed into something that would change him.

56

A photograph from many years before showed him with a wife, the first, and a daughter, the eldest, though she was not elder than anyone back then, but younger than everyone, just a child, and they were in procession, the three of them, and the daughter carried a stuffed animal, a little white dog with black buttons for eyes, and the wife was next, with a dress as white as the dog and an expression of serene victory, and he, the husband, the father, was bringing up the rear, looking rushed, overcoat awry, a package in his hands coming unwrapped, his expression almost an apology for the way things were falling apart but also a statement of intent, especially in the way he looked hungrily forward to the two women, or rather to the woman and the girl. He had an appetite for life and they were part of that life, there was to be no doubt about that. What was in the package? He didn't remember. Probably a steak. He carried steaks around all the time back then.

57

If he hadn't been immensely successful, he would have opened up a little store, maybe a bike shop, maybe dry goods, worked behind the counter greeting people, made sales with a smile on his face, opened a second store and then a third, marketed himself aggressively, driven out the competition, franchised nationally, built a retail empire, gone public, and been immensely successful.

58

His daughter was resplendent in a white dress. It was her word, “resplendent,” and she kept using it, over and over again, like she had seen it on TV or something made him take her to a play. “If you’re going to lead, you have to appear cultured,” she said. It was boring times ten, some violence to spice things up but mostly just a guy talking to a ghost and then later talking to a skull. The skull reminded him of Rudy, and when he turned to tell his daughter, she wasn’t there in the seat next to him, and in her place was a glowing skeleton in that resplendent white dress. He opened his mouth to scream and that’s when he woke up. He should have known it was a dream. Why would he agree to go to a play where they were barely even speaking his language?

59

Once he commissioned a company to see what his name was in different languages, as a word, in case he enjoyed more global expansion. In Spanish, his name was *triunfo*, which reminded him of the English word for victory, which he liked. In Afrikaans, it was *troef*, which reminded his smart son-in-law of the Yiddish word for foods that weren't kosher, and which, for his smart son-in-law's sake, he disliked. In Turkish, it was *gölgede bırakmak*, which was confusing. In Esperanto, it was *trumpetsono*, which seemed trivial, but what was Esperanto anyway? It sounded like a kind of coffee. In Russian, it was *козырять*, a word he stared at for a while. The letters were shaped differently than letters he was used to, but he thought he saw something in them, one man sitting at a table while another man came to offer him secret information, and then, near the first man, a seated woman who was big up top. It was a beautiful language.

60

A sharp word said in anger near a granddaughter led to a reproachful look from a daughter led to a quiet car ride with a son-in-law. A conversation about family with a running mate led to a lecture about realpolitik to a campaign manager led to a late-night phone call with a friend. An investment made in secret with a banker led to an article in a newspaper led to an investigation by a legislative body led to a crisis in the administration led to a sharp word said in anger near a granddaughter.

61

People were always talking about "give and take," but he thought that "take and give" made much more sense, just in case something interrupted the process midway through.

62

On one long rainy afternoon, he could not make the things on his desk do his bidding. A pen wrote skittishly. A stapler jammed. The buttons on the phone were gummed up—they wouldn't go down, and once down they wouldn't come back up. A tiny toy car that he was given as a gift by a prominent auto executive would no longer roll, thanks to a bum rear wheel, and just dragged in a circle. He pushed his chair away from his desk in frustration and went out into his office, where he could find people and yell at them. They would do what he said. People were the best.

63

The art he liked was mostly statues and portraits. They showed you what was already important. They were necessary reminders. He liked photographs of big buildings, too. And historical paintings, if they were also about things that were already important. Other art confused him because it was about crowds and how they moved, or details he didn't need, or lowlifes. That art was about other people, different kinds of people. It seemed like a waste of time. That is one thing he plans to change while he is in charge. More statues, more portraits, less of whatever you'd call the rest of it.

64

He read an article that said the most insightful people learned from literature, and for a second he felt bad. Literature wasn't his thing. Books were stupid, and none stupider than novels. But then he remembered one that had affected him deeply. It was about a singer recalling his wedding with his girlfriend, and also her death after their marriage. She was a beautiful girl, a model. Her wedding dress was short in front. He identified with the singer and his pain. Novels gave you empathy and empathy was what he was filled with, if that's what was needed to feel superior to other people. Later on, an employee told him the novel he was describing was actually the video for Guns N' Roses' "November Rain." He stared at the man. "It was a book," he said. "A novel."

65

Borders, said a scientist on the television, touching the tips of his index fingers together thoughtfully, were just lines on maps, or maybe only ideas in the minds of those people looking at those maps. He was watching the scientist only casually, mostly focused on another screen that was reshowing one of his speeches from a few days earlier, but the thing about borders got his attention. “Hey,” he said to the television, “that’s a stupid idea, so stupid, so so stupid.” Later on, he would insist that the man on the screen paused for a split second, feeling the force of his disapproval.

66

Sometimes he saw footsteps. He didn't hear them. He saw them. They were in the hallway, in the street, in the airplane, glowing. They looked like his shoe prints, high-priced shoes, but in areas of the hall, street, or plane he did not remember going. Were they ghosts? Were they alternatives? Were they predictions? He blinked, and, when that didn't work, juddered his head until he couldn't see them anymore.

67

He did not have many dreams he considered beautiful. Beautiful was a word best reserved for women, or buildings, or deals. But one dream remained with him for a long time. He was in the forest, starting to worry that he didn't know which way was out, when he heard the rush of water. He moved toward it and passed through a clutch of trees into an opening. There was a river moving madly. He walked to the bank and looked over. Everything he saw was foam.

68

He would never have admitted it if asked, but on days when he felt especially low, when some piece of criticism had hit him at more than a superficial level, or he wondered if his contributions to the world would last after he was gone, he imagined that objects around his house were talking to him. “You can’t doubt yourself,” the lamp said. “You’ve got one of the best business minds ever and you’re a quick study in other things, too,” said the armchair. “No one else could have done this,” said the china closet. “You’re a real prince,” the dining room table said, not at all sarcastically.

69

He knew what he was supposed to think about snow. He was supposed to find it beautiful, to see the crystals as examples of magic and mystery, first filling the air, then blanketing the ground. If a child or a very old person asked him, he might say that was what he saw. But if another adult asked him, he would drop his voice to a loud whisper and confess that all he saw was a stretch of road that would have to be cleared, salt going down that might damage the undercarriages of cars, people walking who could slip on ice and then retain personal injury attorneys, chimneys that might have flues that were obstructed. And he didn't see any of those things as problems. He saw them as promise and as profit—if not for him, then for someone else, maybe someone who would later transact business with him in a way that worked to his advantage. His eyes twinkled. Snow really was a beautiful thing.

70

Some people thought the best shape was the circle, or the square, or the oval, or the rectangle, or the star, or the triangle, or the diamond, or the octagon, or the heart, or the teardrop, or the thing that happened when you opened up an umbrella, or the whirlpool, or the pyramid, or the cone. All of them were wrong, all of those people. None of those was the best, none of those shapes. The best shape was the plume.

71

People said that he wasn't a good lister, which was crazy, made no sense: He could list all his properties, all his children, all his wives, all the people who had insulted him on Twitter. Oh. They were saying he wasn't a good listener? That was crazy, too.

72

If he tried hard enough, he could find his reflection everywhere—not just in mirrors and windows and the lenses of people's glasses, but in hundreds of other places. Most metals gave him back at least a hint of his image: the curved stainless steel of a doorknob, the flank of a passing bus, the flat of a table knife. Coins thwarted him in this respect, but he learned to see himself in them in other ways.

73

Sometimes a thing that was not true in the morning was true in the afternoon. Nothing had happened to change its status except that he felt differently about it. Wasn't that what physicists meant when they talked about Schrödinger's cat, that a thing could be not true and then true because a person with lots of money and power had changed his opinion about that thing? He asked a physicist one morning, who said that it was absolutely not the case, but by the afternoon, he had forgotten everything the physicist had said and decided it was absolutely the case.

74

He liked sports. He liked movies. He liked shoes. He liked overcoats. He liked rings, oversize but not gaudily so. He liked magazines, depending who was on the cover. He liked paintings for the same reason. He liked the Bible, from what he had heard—lots of good advice about who to listen to and who to avoid. He liked the country and everything about it. He had mixed feeling about books, though. People filled shelves with them and they overwhelmed the room, because each of them made a case that they wanted your attention. Books weren't like gilt-framed mirrors. You couldn't just put them everywhere.

75

All of his kids were thus far on their first wives or husbands. When they were all together for his big event, he began to feel uneasy about the situation. It was against nature. It created unrealistic expectations. He forced himself to think forward in time to the moment when one of them would announce that things were changing. Explanations would be given. Excuses would be made. Maybe a tear or two would fall. He would sit implacable, thinking backward in time to the moment when he thought about how he once feared that it would never come to this.

76

He used Sharpies because they were all about confidence and certanty.

77

Over the years, magazines and newspapers and television stations and radio stations had created various lists of the planet's most influential people, and every time they left him out, which was every time, it reminded him to check if the little pilot light within him was still lit. It always was, a blue dot in the black void of insufficient recognition. Still within himself, he turned the igniter, heard the click, and waited for the flame to appear. The purpose of that flame, as he knew, as he was happy to tell anyone who asked (as he was happy, in fact, to tell everyone, whether or not they had asked), was to touch it to the bottom of the lists that had left him out and then watch them as they burned. When he was finally included on a list, when he was finally included on them all, he turned the flame down until it was only a source of warmth.

78

Some genius in the press had the theory that he was performing himself—not that he himself was performing, but that his very existence was a performance, that he was at once performer and role, and that everyone else was the audience, the whole country, the whole world, the whole of history. He could not comment on that theory except to say that it was either ridiculous or absolutely true, and that while he was thinking about whether it was ridiculous or true he paced back and forth across his office, bowing his head, lifting it, sometimes raising his arms above his head and shaking his fists at the sky in a silent pantomime of rage. And . . . scene.

79

People kept throwing this word around—*quality*—like it was something magical, and like he didn't have any of the magic that it described, but really all the word meant was an attribute or trait, so anything could be a quality. In a school, courses being unenlightening could be their quality. In a souvenir shop, products being overpriced could be their quality. In a restaurant, dishes being unpalatable could be their quality. He patted the dictionary, his friend for now.

80

Traveling across America, some towns smelled liked rubber. Some towns smelled like eggs. Some towns didn't smell like anything, because he was holding his breath until he was out of there, away from the small sour buildings and smaller sourer faces in their windows. Once, he came around a corner early in the morning, his mind still a little bit back on the airplane, when he had been firing off deal points on the phone, and still a little bit on the night before, when his beautiful wife had come to him clothed only in expensive lingerie and taken it off theatrically, he came around a corner and saw what looked like an army unit, a row of jeeps, one big vehicle that was some kind of armored something, and soldiers standing straight beside anything with wheels. It was all dark green, all the machines, all the men. He banished memories of the plane and the bedroom and breathed in as much of the town as he could. It smelled familiar. It smelled like clout.

81

At the opening of a golf course in Australia, an Indian he had met once or twice, a telecom billionaire he generally avoided because the Indian's wealth had inched past his own, approached him with the wide smile of a man who knew it. "Hello!" the Indian said. Silence descended. The Indian sensed it. Anyone would have. But his good cheer was not to be denied. "I have a riddle for you," the Indian said. "Poor people have it. Rich people need it. If you eat it, you perish. What is it?" Despite himself, he was intrigued by the Indian's riddle. "What?" he grunted. A twinkle rose into the Indian's eye. "Nothing," the Indian said. The Indian clapped him on the back and strode off down the twelfth green.

82

The sound in an airplane cabin was like nothing else, a clean set of frequencies, engines and hydraulics polishing the air. It was the closest thing to meditation he had ever known. He tried to explain it to Rudy, but Rudy thought he was saying medication and sprinted off down a path of beta blockers and prostate surgery and Viagra and Anthony Weiner, after which he did an imitation of one of the pictures Weiner had taken, and that occasioned a joke about Geraldo's shirtless selfie, and that tumbled into a discussion of how the whole Jerry Rivers thing wasn't really true, that Rivera was Geraldo's real last name even though he was half-Jewish but that his family switched to Rivers because of discrimination, and that brought them to the foot of the wall, and how it wasn't a hateful thing at all, that a country without laws was no country at all. He turned to Reince, who was on the other side of him. "Make Rudy shut up," he said. Reince's brow furrowed. "Rudy's not on this flight," he said, and he was right, and Reince wasn't on the flight either. He was alone, save for the pilot, and his own thoughts filled the cabin, drowning out everything, even the clean frequencies of the engines and hydraulics as they polished the air.

83

He used to use his landline, but now he doesn't trust it. You never know who might be listening in. He used to use the cell phone, but now he doesn't trust it. That's even less secure than a landline: towers and frequencies and bands. He used to use email, but now he doesn't trust it. Your messages could be plucked off a server by disreputable types and sent around the world to laughing enemies. He used to use the U.S. mail, but now he doesn't trust it. The guy lurking across the street in the navy blue windbreaker could take the mailman down with a karate chop and steal your letters. Keeping communication secret is absolutely paramount. It's vital that it not fall into hostile hands. That's why he has no choice but to use Twitter.

84

Newspapers were always using the worst pictures of him. Why couldn't they find the ones where he stared with smoldering magnetism into the camera, his body descending from muscular chest to trim waist in a perfect V-taper? Why couldn't they find the one where he was taking mankind's first step on the moon, or the one where he and five other Marines were raising the U.S. flag atop Mount Suribachi? People who found photos were like people who wrote words: lazy, petty, and, like the pictures they found, the worst.

85

Had you followed him late at night, you would have seen him wake, throw on a thick robe, and walk slowly down the hall from his bedroom to his office, where he took a seat in a large chair, brought out a large ledger-book, and opened it on his lap. He would have studied page after page, sometimes nodding, sometimes shaking his head, sometimes letting go a small noise that signified satisfaction. What he was looking for wasn't only evidence of his wealth, though he found it, but evidence of negotiations where he had thoroughly bested others in deals. He wanted to see a good number on his side, and a bad number on the other side. In rare occasions, the noise that escaped him conveyed not satisfaction but a kind of existential sorrow that came from the fact that he was up late at night looking through the ledger-book while others—in the world and even in his home, down the hall—slept soundly, dreaming human dreams.

86

For years he read interviews with politicians who said that they liked to watch history documentaries when they couldn't sleep. It was their way of saying they were always in tune with civilization's largest currents: wars and inventions, famines and industrialists. He liked those channels fine. But when push came to shove, you couldn't beat a good tabloid show. The startled look in the eyes of aging musicians ambushed by cameras, the merciless scrutiny of young starlets and their surgeries, the glory and humiliation, and the glory of humiliation. Those were his wars and inventions.

87

"I am not a puppet," said the man. "I am a puppeteer." He tugged at the strings connected to his hands and below him a puppet leapt into the air, limbs suddenly alive. The camera pulled back to show a larger man standing above the man. "I am not a puppet," said the larger man. "I am a puppeteer." He tugged at the strings connected to his hands and below him the man leapt into the air, limbs suddenly alive. The camera pulled back to show an even larger man. "I am not a puppet," said the even larger man. "I am a puppeteer." He tugged at the strings connected to his hands and below him the larger man leapt into the air, limbs suddenly alive. The show never ended, though it had moments where it was suspended occasionally so that men of various sizes could rest, take sips of water, run for public office. "Is this metaphor too on the nose?" the man asked when the show resumed. The larger man above him moved his hands and the man's head shook from side to side, indicating no.

88

The news was sordid. He was the news. But he wasn't sordid. He was wonderful. The news wasn't wonderful. But he was the news. The news was shocking. He was shocking. But that wasn't news. The news wasn't false. But he wasn't false. He was true. That made no sense. The news made no sense. But he made no sense. He was the news.

89

So angry. He had gone to sleep angry, partly because of the media—they were always after him, always hounding him—but also because of his staff, who wouldn't listen; and his knee, which felt sore; and his stomach, which felt sour. Time passed and you got worse and the people around you got worse, too. Why wouldn't that make you angry? He had gone to sleep angry and then he had woken up angrier, with a faint memory of a bad dream, and the morning had just snowballed, one piece of news after another, good people being maligned, bad people gloating on TV, an aide shoving a piece of paper in his face and telling him to read it. "You read it!" he shouted. "I don't read." Now his secret was out, which made him even angrier yet again.

90

He always assumed he was being recorded, which is why he recorded everyone, too. Two recordings cancelled each other out, and then there were no recordings, right? Wasn't that how it worked? He had a book that explained all those things, an electronics textbook, but it was on the far side of the bathroom, and he wasn't about to stand up from the toilet and walk over there to get it.

91

Loyalty wasn't a two-way street. It wasn't even a one-way street. It was a no-way street, sealed off on both ends, with a single house in the middle of the block, and he was sitting on a lawn chair in the front yard, talking to a friend who was sitting in an identical lawn chair, the two of them sipping iced tea as the house burned.

92

"Did you really think you could get away with it?" He couldn't believe it. He was being challenged right there in the lobby of his building in New York. He started to turn toward the voice, a woman's voice, as he formulated a response. Maybe he'd shake a fist at her. Maybe he'd shrug, that clumsy poor-me shrug that sometimes got people laughing. Maybe he'd tell her that she looked terrific, if she looked terrific. As he turned, he saw that the woman wasn't talking to him. She was talking to her dog, which had some kind of granola bar in its mouth. Who let the dog in the building? The lady did look terrific, though.

93

In a hotel room in a distant country whose name he wasn't sure how to pronounce, there was a copy of *Gulliver's Travels* by Jonathan Swift, and he looked at the cover, which showed a giant being tied down by tiny beings. For my next book, he thought, I'm going to use that as the cover image. He made a mental note to call this Swift guy and buy the cover picture from him, no matter what it cost. Every man had his price.

94

A dark hill. A dark hill at night. A dark hill at night ringed by skulls. A dark hill at night ringed by skulls whose mouths still spoke. Some spoke ceaselessly, others infrequently, all with a mix of invective and praise: You're the worst, you're food for worms, you're the best, you should lead them all, your days are numbered, that number is large, you belong with us, you belong to history. The few skulls that did not speak had coins in their eyes, coins whose denominations he could not see.

95

People complained that there already was a Great Wall, but his wall would work hard to earn the designation. He would build it across the nation's entire border to protect against invading immigrants. He would use stone, brick, wood, and tamped earth. He would install battlements with parapets that would permit guards to watch over the surrounding land. He would ensure it exceeded ten thousand miles in length but leave it to archaeological surveys to determine the exact number. He would begin construction as early as the seventh century B.C., add sections over time, and finish between the fourteenth and seventeenth centuries. He would spray-paint it all gold.

96

He was off on another rally, speaking to a large crowd, making all the usual points, who was bad, who was good, who was going to be so happy, who was going to be sorry, when he saw a middle-aged woman with glasses holding up a sign. NOT EVERY ANGRY MAN IS A MADMAN, it said, and there was a picture of him. He didn't know what the sign meant, and because of that he didn't like it. He didn't know whether the woman was defending him, or questioning whether or not his anger was genuine, or acknowledging that it was genuine but claiming it didn't have any real power behind it. He was genuinely angry at the sign, and he considered ripping it from the hand of the woman who was holding it, throwing it to the ground, stomping on it, and then ordering that it be burned until it was only ashes drifting in the air, but he wasn't about to do anything crazy. He concluded his speech and made sure to pass by the woman with the sign as he exited the venue, so that he could mutter something unkind just loud enough for her to hear. "Four-eyes," he said. "Nerd. Harry Potter."

97

One night he took off his jacket and didn't stop there, or at tie, or at shirt, or at pants, or at undershirt, or at underwear, or at hair, or at skin, or at teeth, or at bones. He popped out his eyes, set them a short distance from where he stood, and looked back at himself. What he saw—all he saw—was a wave of will, a machine designed to take offense, a mover of men, a boldface name. And people said he wasn't introspective.

98

Presidents had legacies. The late great Abraham Lincoln had the Emancipation Proclamation. The late great Harry S. Truman had the Marshall Plan. The late great Thomas Jefferson had the Louisiana Purchase. He wasn't late yet but he could start to plan for being great. Would it be a war? The taking of land that was not previously American? A new letter in the movie ratings system? Figuring out what was happening to all those bees? He had already created a company under his granddaughter's name, Arabella Holdings, and instructed that a surveyor be dispatched to South Dakota to measure the rock face next to Lincoln. Legacy to be determined.

99

When he was a very old man, well past ninety, cresting the hill of an age he never imagined he'd reach, he told his great-grandchildren stories about how things used to be. He told them about how there had once been many countries, and many hostilities between them, before they had all found common purpose. He told them about how there had been divisions on earth between different religions and races before the rising waters forced them all to bond together. He told them about when he lived on the sixty-eighth floor of a building, hundreds of feet lower than now they lived, and traveled by automobile rather than just boat and plane. He told them about how there had once been men and women entrusted with holding the powerful accountable, and newspapers and magazines that carried their work, before some were thrown in jail and others went into hiding. The scarier the stories, the more his great-grandchildren liked them. In that, they took after him.

100

The belief that every story ended with a beginning was for New Agers and eggheads. It let them keep their heads in the clouds. He knew the truth, which was that every story ended with an end.

101

There are no pearly gates, only a long circular conveyor belt where you pick up your luggage. It has been years since he had to do that. Glowing boxes come around the belt, each a slightly different color. The people on the perimeter of the belt move slowly toward him, their faces not quite in focus. He senses that they are avoiding him, but also that they are in pain. Maybe he, too, is in pain? He feels his legs taking him in the direction of a large gray-blue box: the largest. As he approaches the box, it begins to hum, a dull hum that sharpens the closer he gets. A light that is not a lightness wreathes him.

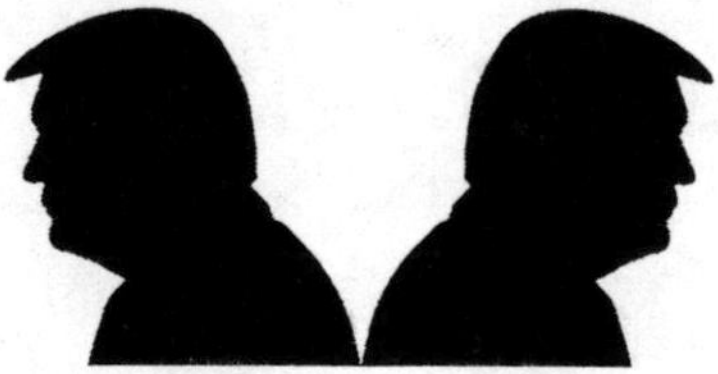

About the Author

Ben Greenman is a *New York Times*–bestselling author who has written both nonfiction and fiction. He is the author of several acclaimed works of fiction, including the novel *The Slippage* and the short-story collections *What He's Poised to Do* and *Superbad*. He is the co-author of the bestselling *Mo' Meta Blues* with Questlove, the bestselling *I Am Brian Wilson* with Brian Wilson, *Brothas Be, Yo Like George, Ain't That Funkin' Kinda Hard on You?* with George Clinton, and more. His fiction, essays, and journalism have appeared in the *New Yorker*, the *New York Times*, the *Washington Post*, the *Paris Review*, *Zoetrope: All-Story*, *McSweeney's*, and elsewhere, and have been widely anthologized. His most recent book is *Dig If You Will The Picture*, a meditation on the life and career of Prince.